All Bible verses taken from the King James
Version of the Bible, unless otherwise
indicated.

First Printing 2003
Second Printing 2023

ISBN: 978-1-960150-54-7
Paperback Version

got HOPE?

got HOPE?
Verses for Life

Freshwater

got HOPE?
HOPE is the expectation of Good.

Got HOPE?
There is nothing so well known as that we
should not expect something for nothing, but
we all do and call it HOPE.
Edgar Watson Howe

got HOPE?
HOPE is a good breakfast, but it is a bad
supper.
Francis Bacon 1624

got HOPE?
You got up this morning because of
HOPE.
You showered because of HOPE.
You have HOPE.

Got HOPE?
Hope springs eternal.
Alexander Pope

got HOPE?
As long as God is forgiving...there is
HOPE.
Ezra 10:2

got HOPE?
As long as there is life, there is HOPE.

got HOPE?
HOPE sees the invisible, feels the
intangible, and achieves the impossible.
Helen Keller

got HOPE?
Is not your [reverent] fear of God your
confidence and the integrity and
uprightness of your ways your HOPE?
Job 4:6, AMP

got HOPE?
Those who forget God have no HOPE.
Job 8:23a

got HOPE?
HOPE is being able to see that there is
light despite all of the darkness.
Desmond Tutu

got HOPE?
The HOPE of a man who has forgotten
God will be cut off.
Job 8:14

got HOPE?
The wicked's only HOPE is dying.
Job 11:20

got HOPE?
If a tree is cut down there is HOPE that
it will sprout again.
Despise not the pruning of the LORD.
Job 14:7

got HOPE?
The godless have no HOPE.
Job 27:8

got HOPE?
Therefore my heart is glad, and my
glory rejoices;
My flesh also will rest in HOPE.
Psalm 16:9, NKJV

got HOPE?
I HOPED when I was on my mother's
breasts.
Psalm 22:19

got HOPE?
Be of good courage, and he shall
strengthen your heart, all ye that HOPE
in the LORD.
Psalm 31:24

got HOPE?
HOPE in the Mercy of the LORD and
He will keep His eye upon you.
Psalm 33:18; 33:22

got HOPE?
I believe that imagination is stronger
than knowledge. That myth is more
potent than history. That dreams are
more powerful than facts. That HOPE
always triumphs over experience. That
laughter is the only cure for grief. And
I believe that love is stronger than
death.
Robert Fulghum

got HOPE?

My HOPE is built on nothing less, then
Jesus' Blood and Righteousness.
(Hymn)

got HOPE?

HOPE in God and praise Him for the
help of His countenance.
Psalm 42:5

got HOPE?

HOPE in the LORD;
praise Him for He is the health to your
countenance.
Psalm 42:11; 43:5

got HOPE?
For thou art my HOPE, O Lord GOD:
thou art my trust from my youth.
By thee have I been holden up from the
womb:
thou art he that took me out of my
mother's bowels:
my praise shall be continually of thee.
Psalm 71:5-6

got HOPE?
HOPE continually and praise God
more and more.
Psalm 71:14

got HOPE?
Set your HOPE in God.
Psalm 78:7

got HOPE?
Then you must have a Word from God.

Got HOPE?
God's Word will cause you to HOPE.
Psalm 119:49; 119:81

got HOPE?
Thou art my hiding place and my
shield:
I HOPE in thy Word.
Psalm 119:114

got HOPE?
Uphold me according to thy promise,
that I may live, and let me not be put to
shame in my HOPE!
Psalm 119:116, RSV

got HOPE?
My HOPE is in the LORD.
Psalm 39:7

got HOPE?
And in His Word do I HOPE.
My soul waits for the Lord
More than the watchmen for the
morning; Indeed, more than the
watchmen for the morning.
Psalm 130:5-6, NAS

got HOPE?

O Israel, HOPE in the LORD;
for with the LORD there is
lovingkindness,
and with Him is abundant redemption.
And He will redeem Israel
from all his iniquities
Psalm 130:7-8, NAS

got HOPE?

Then you are blessed.
Blessed is the man
whose HOPE is in the LORD.
Psalm 146:5

got HOPE?
The HOPE of the Righteous is gladness.
got JOY?
Proverbs 10:28
(Read *got JOY?* by Dr. Marlene Miles)

got HOPE?
Then you've got favor.
God favors those who HOPE in Him.
Psalm 147:11

got HOPE?
HOPE deferred maketh the heart sick:
but when the desire cometh, it is a tree
of life.
Proverbs 13:12

got HOPE?
The Righteous have HOPE
when a wicked man dies.
Proverbs 14:32

got HOPE?
Chasten thy son while there is HOPE
and let not thy soul spare for his
crying.
Proverbs 19:18

got HOPE?
Anyone who is among the living has
HOPE-even a live dog is better off than
a dead lion!
Ecclesiastes 9:4, NIV

got HOPE?
Those who go down into the pit cannot
HOPE for God's Truth. Get the Truth
while it can be found.
Isaiah 38:18

got HOPE?
You were wearied with the length of
your way,
but you did not say, *"It is hopeless,"*
you found new life for your strength,
and so you were not faint.
Isaiah 57:10, RSV

got HOPE?
Jesus, The HOPE of Israel.

got HOPE?
Jesus, the God of HOPE.

Got HOPE?
Most] blessed is the man who believes
in, trusts in,
and relies on the Lord, and whose
HOPE and
confidence the Lord is.
For he shall be like a tree planted by
the waters that spreads out its roots by
the river; and it shall not see
and fear when heat comes; but its leaf
shall be green. It shall not be anxious
and full of care in the year of drought,
nor shall it cease yielding fruit.
Jeremiah 17:7-8, AMP

got HOPE?

O LORD, the HOPE of Israel,
All who forsake Thee will be put to
shame.
Those who turn away on earth will be
written down,
Because they have forsaken the
fountain of living water, even the
LORD.
Jeremiah 17:13, NAS

got HOPE?

My HOPE is in the name of Jesus.
(song Eddie James)

got HOPE?
The LORD is your HOPE in the day of
evil.
Jeremiah 17:17

got HOPE?
Yet this I call to mind
and therefore I have HOPE:
Because of the LORD's great love we
are not consumed,
for his compassions never fail.
They are new every morning;
great is your faithfulness.
I say to myself, *"The LORD is my
portion;
therefore I will wait for him."*
Lamentations 3:21-24, NIV

got HOPE?

It is good that a man should both HOPE
and quietly wait for the salvation of the
LORD.

Lamentations 3:26

got HOPE?

Have the Prophet to prophesy to the
dry bones,
that you may have HOPE.

Ezekiel 37:11

got HOPE?

...the valley of Achor for a door of
HOPE.

Hosea 2:15

got HOPE?

The LORD will be the HOPE of His
people.
Joel 3:16

got HOPE?

Turn you to the strong hold, ye
prisoners of HOPE:
even today do I declare that I will
render
double unto thee;
Zechariah 9:12

got HOPE?

There is HOPE toward God that there is
resurrection.

Acts 24:15

got HOPE?

HOPE is the cause that helps you
endure hardship.

Acts 28:20

got HOPE?
Then your heart is glad and you
rejoice.
Acts 2:26

got HOPE?
Who against HOPE believed in HOPE,
that he might become the father of
many nations; according to that which
was spoken, So shall thy seed be.
Romans 4:18

got HOPE?

Rejoice in the HOPE of the Glory of
God.

Romans 5:2

got HOPE?

I believe that anyone can conquer fear
by doing the things he fears to do,
provided he keeps doing them until he
gets a record of successful
experiences behind him.

Eleanor Roosevelt

got HOPE?
...and HOPE does not disappoint,
because the love of God has been
poured out within our hearts through
the Holy Spirit who was given to us.
Romans 5:5, NASU

got HOPE?
The LORD: The HOPE of your fathers.
Jeremiah 50:7

got HOPE?
We are God's creation,
and we have been subjected to HOPE.
Romans 8:20

got HOPE?

For we are saved by HOPE: but HOPE that is seen is not HOPE: for what a man seeth, why doth he yet HOPE for? But if we HOPE for that we see not, then do we with patience wait for it.
Romans 8:24-25

got HOPE?

Then you rejoice in HOPE, you are patient in tribulation and instant in prayer.
Romans 12:12

got HOPE?
Tribulation works patience. Patience,
experience.
Experience, HOPE.
Romans 5:3-4

got HOPE?
We have HOPE through the patience
and comfort
of the Scriptures.
Romans 15:4

got HOPE?
God is the God of HOPE.
Romans 15:13

got HOPE?
Now the God of HOPE fill you with all
joy and peace in believing, that ye may
abound in hope, through the power of
the Holy Ghost.
Romans 15:13

got HOPE?
He that plows should plow in HOPE.
He that threshes should thresh in HOPE
and
He should also be a partaker of his
HOPE.
1 Corinthians 9:10

got HOPE?
Now abides Faith, HOPE and charity...
1 Corinthians 13:13

got HOPE?
HOPE abides; it comes to live with you.
got HOPE?

got HOPE?
HOPE in Christ.

Got HOPE?
Through the Spirit we wait for the
HOPE of Righteousness, through faith.
Galatians 5:5

got HOPE?
What is the HOPE of Christ's calling in
your life?
Ephesians 1:18

got HOPE?
There is one body, and one Spirit, even
as ye are called in one HOPE of your
calling;
One Lord, one faith, one baptism,
One God and Father of all, who is
above all,
and through all,
and in you all.
Ephesians 4:4-6

got HOPE?
...For the HOPE which is laid up for you
in heaven.
Colossians 1:5

got HOPE?
HOPE does not sorrow.
1 Thessalonians 4:13

got HOPE?
Do not be moved from the HOPE of the
Gospel.
Colossians 1:23

got HOPE?
Christ in you, the HOPE of Glory.
Colossians 1:27

got HOPE?
Be patient in your HOPE.

Got HOPE?
For what is our HOPE, or joy, or crown
of rejoicing?
Are not even ye in the presence of our
Lord Jesus Christ at His coming?
For ye are our glory and joy.
1 Thessalonians 2:19-20

got HOPE?
Put on the HOPE of salvation for a
helmet.
1 Thessalonians 5:8

got HOPE?
Now our Lord Jesus Christ himself, and
God,
even our Father,
which hath loved us, and hath given us
everlasting consolation and good HOPE
through grace. (*got GRACE?*)
2 Thessalonians 2:16

got HOPE?

In HOPE of eternal life, which God,
that cannot lie,
promised before the world began;
Titus 1:2

got HOPE?

Blessed HOPE: The glorious appearing
of the great God and our Savior Jesus
Christ.
Titus 2:13

got HOPE?

We are heirs according to the HOPE of
eternal life.

Titus 3:7

got HOPE?

Lay hold upon the HOPE set before us:

Hebrews 6:18

got HOPE?

HOPE anchors our souls.

Hebrews 6:19

got HOPE?
Jesus: the Better HOPE.
Hebrews 7:19

got HOPE?
Jesus Christ resurrected from the dead
gives us a lively HOPE.
1 Peter 1:3

got HOPE?
And every man that hath this
HOPE in him
purifieth himself, even as He is pure.
1 John 3:3

got HOPE?

Wherefore gird up the loins of your
mind, be sober, and HOPE to the end
for the grace that is to be brought unto
you at the revelation of Jesus Christ;
As obedient children, not fashioning
yourselves according to the former
lusts in your ignorance:
But as he which hath called you is holy,
so be ye holy in all manner of
conversation;
Because it is written, Be ye holy; for I
am holy.
1 Peter 1:13-16

got HOPE?

But sanctify the Lord God in your
hearts: and be ready always to give an
answer to every man that asketh you a
reason of the HOPE that is in you with
meekness and fear:

Having a good conscience; that,
whereas they speak evil of you, as of
evildoers, they may be ashamed that
falsely accuse your good conversation
in Christ.

1 Peter 3:15-16

got HOPE?
Love beareth all things, believeth all
things, HOPETH all things, endureth all
things.
got LOVE?
1 Corinthians 13:7
(Read *got LOVE?* by this author.)

got HOPE?
It is vain to HOPE for salvation from
the hills.
My help comes from the LORD.
Jeremiah 3:23 and Psalm 121:1-3

got HOPE?
HOPE comes from the LORD.
Psalm 39:7

got HOPE?
HOPE comes from the calling of God.
Ephesians 1:18; 4:4

got HOPE?
HOPE comes from the GRACE of God.
Got GRACE?
2 Thessalonians 2:16

got HOPE?

Christ never spoke the word, HOPE
because He was filled with certainty.
We are human, but should be filled
with Christ, therefore we HOPE until
Faith comes.

Got HOPE?

Faith is the big brother of HOPE; Christ
is our "big brother."

got HOPE?
Christ, our Living HOPE.

Got HOPE?
HOPE
"we have fixed our HOPE on the living
God, who is the Savior of all men"
(1 Tim 4:10 NAS)

got HOPE?
HOPE makes life doable and the future bright.

Got HOPE?
Cease, every joy, to glimmer on my mind,
But leave~~~oh! Leave the light of HOPE behind.
Thomas Campbell

got HOPE?
Gratitude is merely the secret hope of further favors.
Francois de La Rochefoucauld

got HOPE?

Appetite, with an opinion of attaining,
is called hope; the same, without such
opinion,
despair.
Thomas Hobbes

got HOPE?

I am counting on the LORD, yes, I am
counting on him. I have put my HOPE
in his Word.
Psalm 130:5

got HOPE?
Whoever does not love his work cannot
hope that it will please others.
Unknown

got HOPE?
You are not here merely to make a
living. You are here to enable the world
to live more amply, with greater vision,
and with a finer *spirit of HOPE* and
achievement. You
are here to enrich the world. You
impoverish yourself if you forget this
errand.
Woodrow Wilson

got HOPE?
What we HOPE ever to do with ease we
may learn first to do with diligence.
Samuel Johnson, *Lives of the Poets*

got HOPE?
Our imagination is the only limit to
what we can HOPE to have in the
future.
Charles F. Kettering

got HOPE?
It is difficult to say what is impossible,
for the dream of yesterday is the HOPE
of today and the reality of tomorrow.
Robert H. Goddard

got HOPE?
Make no little plans; they have no
magic to stir men's blood...
Make big plans, aim high
in HOPE and work.
Daniel H. Burnham

got HOPE?
Do not spoil what you have by desiring
what you have not; but remember that
what you now have was once among
the things only HOPED for.
Epicurus

got HOPE?
A sailor without a destination cannot
HOPE for a favorable wind.
Leon Tec, M.D.

got HOPE?
If you wish success in life, make
perseverance your bosom friend,
experience your
wise counselor, caution your elder
brother and hope your guardian
genius.
Joseph Addison

got HOPE?

It was never what I wanted to buy that held my heart's HOPE. It was what I wanted to be.

Lois McMaster Bujold

got HOPE?

And so at last the poor have HOPE, and the fangs of the wicked are broken.

Job 5:16 TLB

got HOPE?
The past is a source of knowledge, and
the future is a source of HOPE.
Love of the past
implies faith in the future.
Stephen Ambrose

got HOPE?
I know how men in exile feed on
dreams of HOPE.
Aeschylus, *Agamemnon*

got HOPE?
How can you sing the Lord's song in a
strange land?
Psalm 137:4
HOPE.

Got HOPE?
HOPE is a waking dream.
Aristotle

got HOPE?
While there's life, there's HOPE.
Cicero

got HOPE?

Take HOPE from the heart of man, and
you make him a beast of prey.

Quida

got HOPE?

I HOPE that while so many people are
out smelling the flowers, someone is
taking the
time to plant some.

Herbert Rappaport

got HOPE?

It was the best of times, it was the
worst of times, it was the age of
wisdom, it was the
age of foolishness, it was the epoch of
belief, it was the epoch of incredulity, it
was the
season of Light, it was the season of
Darkness, it was the spring of HOPE, it
was the
winter of despair, we had everything
before us, we had nothing before us,
we were all
going direct to heaven, we were all

doing direct the other way – in short,
the period
was so far like the present period, that
some of its noisiest authorities insisted
on its
being received, for good or for evil, in
the superlative degree of comparison
only.
Charles Dickens, *A Tale of Two Cities*

got HOPE?
He who has never HOPED can never
despair.
George Bernard Shaw

got HOPE?
Never deprive someone of HOPE – it
may be all they have.
Unknown

got HOPE?
Most of the important things in the
world have been accomplished by
people who have
kept on trying when there seemed to be
no HOPE at all.
Dale Carnegie

got HOPE?
Intercessors live on HOPE.

Got HOPE?
Make no little plans; they have no
magic to stir men's blood and probably
will
themselves not be realized. Make big
plans; aim high in HOPE and work,
remembering
that a noble, logical diagram once
recorded will not die.
Daniel Burnham

got HOPE?

It is from numberless diverse acts of
courage and belief that human history
is shaped.
Each time a man stands up for an ideal,
or acts to improve the lot of others, or
strikes
out against injustice, he sends forth a
tiny ripple of HOPE, and crossing each
other from
a million different centers of energy
and daring, those ripples build a
current that can
sweep down the mightiest walls of
oppression and resistance.
Robert F. Kennedy

got HOPE?
If money is your HOPE for
independence, you will never have it.
The only real security
that a man will have in this world is a
reserve of knowledge, experience, and
ability.
Henry Ford

got HOPE?
HOPE, like faith, is nothing if it is not
courageous; it is nothing if it is not
ridiculous.
Thornton Wilder

got HOPE?
Keep HOPE alive.
Jessee Jackson

got HOPE?
Women with pasts interest men... they
HOPE history will repeat itself.
Mae West

got HOPE?
Do not put your HOPE in material
things.

got HOPE?

HOPE is the companion of power, and mother of success; for who so HOPES strongly has within him the gift of miracles.

Samuel Smiles

got HOPE?

Where there is no HOPE, there can be no endeavor.

Johnson

got HOPE?

Never lose HOPE.

Unknown, Polish Slogan

got HOPE?
HOPE is the last thing that dies in man;
and though it be exceedingly deceitful,
yet it is
of this good use to us, that while we
are traveling through life it conducts us
in an
easier and more pleasant way to our
journey's end.
Francois De La Rochefoucauld

got HOPE?
We promise according to our HOPES
and perform according to our fears.
Unknown

got HOPE?

He that lives upon HOPE dies fasting.
Benjamin Franklin

got HOPE?

There are many ways of breaking a
heart. Stories were full of hearts
broken by love,
but what really broke a heart was
taking away its dream – whatever that
dream might
be.
Pearl Buck

got HOPE?
Dream, live!
Powerhouse Revival Center CD title.

got HOPE?
HOPE is a state of mind, not of the
world. HOPE, in this deep and
powerful sense, is
not the same as joy that things are
going well, or willingness to invest in
enterprises that are obviously heading
for success, but rather an ability to
work for something
because it is good.
Vaclav Havel

got HOPE?

Never lose HOPE. Storms make people
stronger and never last forever.
Roy T. Bennett

got HOPE?

Every great dream begins with a
dreamer. Always remember, you have
within you the strength, the **patience**,
and the passion to reach for the stars to
change the world.
Harriet Tubman

got HOPE?

To live without HOPE is to cease to live.
Fyodor Dostoyevsky

got HOPE?

Darkness comes. In the middle of it,
the future looks blank. The temptation
to quit is huge. Don't. You are in good
company... You will argue with
yourself that there is no way forward.
But with God, nothing is impossible. He
has more ropes and ladders and
tunnels out of pits than you can
conceive. Wait. Pray without ceasing.
HOPE.
John Pipe

got HOPE?

My country owes me nothing. It gave
me, as it gives every boy and girl, a
chance. It gave me schooling,
independence of action, opportunity
for service and honor. In no
other land could a boy from a country
village, without inheritance or
influential friends,
look forward with unbounded HOPE.
Herbert Hoover

got HOPE?

May your choices reflect your HOPES,
not your fears.
Nelson Mandela

got HOPE?

HOPE is the power of being cheerful in
circumstances that we know to be
desperate.
G.K. Chesterton

got HOPE?

There is no medicine like HOPE, no
incentive so great, and no tonic so
powerful as expectation of something
tomorrow.
O. S. Marden

got HOPE?

When there is HOPE you can be secure.
Job 11:18

got HOPE?

A strong mind always HOPES and has
always cause to HOPE.

Thomas Carlyle

got HOPE?

We have always held to the HOPE, the
belief, the conviction that there is a
better life, a better world, beyond the
horizon.

Franklin D. Roosevelt

got HOPE?

Hang on to your hat.
Hang on to your HOPE.
And wind the clock,
for tomorrow is another day.
E.B. White

got HOPE?

But I know, somehow,
that only when it is dark enough
can you see the stars.
Martin Luther King, Jr.

got HOPE?
The very least you can do in your life is
figure out what you HOPE for.
And the most you can do is live inside
that HOPE.
Not admire it from a distance but live
right in it, under its roof.
Barbara Kingsolver

got HOPE?
No matter where you're from, your
dreams are valid.
Lupita Nyong'o

got HOPE?

Everything that is done in the world is
done by HOPE.
Martin Luther

got HOPE?

When you stop HOPING
you start settling.
Valorie Burton

got HOPE?

HOPE arouses, as nothing else can
arouse, a passion for the possible.
William Sloane Coffin

got HOPE?

HOPE lies in dreams, in imagination,
and in the courage of those who dare
to make dreams into reality.
Jonas Salk

got HOPE?

HOPE itself is like a star—not to be
seen in the sunshine of prosperity,
and only to be discovered in the night
of adversity.
Charles Spurgeon

got HOPE?

Never give up on something that you
can't go a day without thinking about.
Winston Churchill

got HOPE?

The natural flights of the human mind
are not from pleasure to pleasure but
from hope to hope.
Samuel Johnson

got HOPE?

All human wisdom is summed up in
two words; wait and HOPE.
Alexandre Dumas

got HOPE?

When you feel like HOPE is gone, look
inside you and be strong and you'll
finally see the truth—that hero lies in
you.
Mariah Carey

got HOPE?
There are far, far better things ahead
than anything we leave behind.
C. S. Lewis

got HOPE?
We need HOPE,
or else we cannot endure.
Sarah J. Maas

got HOPE?

HOPE is the word which God has written
on the brow of every man.

Victor Hugo

got HOPE?

God's mercy and grace give me HOPE – for
myself, and for our world.

Billy Graham

got HOPE?

We must free ourselves of the HOPE that
the sea will ever rest. We must learn to sail
in high winds.

Aristotle Onassis

got HOPE?

You are never too old to set another goal or
to dream a new dream.

C.S. Lewis

got HOPE?
A whole stack of memories never equal one
little hope.
Charles M. Shultz

got HOPE?
If you have HOPE in the LORD,
He will hear your prayers.
Psalm 38:15

got HOPE?
Those who have HOPE can say,
Heal me, LORD,
I shall be healed.
Save me, LORD, I shall be saved.
Thou art my praise.
Jeremiah 17:13-14

got HOPE?

And if our HOPE in Christ is only for this
life, we are more to be pitied than anyone
in the world.
1 Corinthians 15:19 NLT

got HOPE?

The same happens to all who forget God. The
HOPES of the godless evaporate.
Job 8:13

got HOPE?

In the same way, Wisdom is sweet to your soul.
If you find it, you will have a bright future,
and your HOPES will not be cut short.
Proverbs 24:14NLT

got HOPE?
But I keep praying to you, LORD, HOPING this time you will show me favor. In your unfailing love, O God, answer my prayer with your sure salvation.
Psalm 69:13, NLT

got HOPE?
May integrity and honesty protect me, for I put my HOPE in you.
Psalm 25:21 NLT

got HOPE?
So be strong and courageous, all you who put your HOPE in the LORD
Psalm 31:24 NLT

got HOPE?

We put our HOPE in the LORD. He is our
help and our shield.

Psalm 33:20 NLT

got HOPE?

Let your unfailing love surround us, LORD,
for our HOPE is in You alone.

Psalm 33:32 NLT

got HOPE?

Put your HOPE in the LORD.
Travel steadily along his path.

Psalm 37:34 NLT

got HOPE?

He will honor you by giving you the land.
You will see the wicked destroyed.
Psalm 37:34 NLT

got HOPE?

Life may not be the party we HOPED for,
but while we're here we should dance.
Unknown

got HOPE?

There is HOPE for your future, declares the
LORD.
Jeremiah 31:17

got HOPE?

And so, Lord, where do I put my HOPE?
My only HOPE is in You.
Psalm 39:7 NLT

Christian books by this author:

AK: Adventures of the Agape Kid
AMONG SOME THIEVES
As My Soul Prospers
Behave
Churchzilla (The Wanna-Be Bride of Christ)
The Coco~So~So Correct Show
Demons Hate Questions
Do Not Orphan Your Seed
Do Not Work for Money
Don't Refuse Me Lord
The FAT Demons
got Money?
Let Me Have a Dollar's Worth
Living for the NOW of God
Lord, Help My Debt
Lose My Location
Made Perfect In Love
The Man Safari *(Really, I'm Just Looking)*
Marriage Ed., *Rules of Engagement & Marriage*
The Motherboard: *Key to Soul Prosperity*
My Life As A Slave
Name Your Seed
Plantation Souls
The Poor Attitudes of Money
Power Money: Nine Times the Tithe
The Power of Wealth
Seasons of Grief
Seasons of War

SOULS in Captivity
Soul Prosperity: Your Health & Your Wealth
The *spirit* of Poverty
The Throne of Grace, *Courtroom Prayers*
Warfare Prayer Against Poverty
When the Devourer is Rebuked
The Wilderness Romance

Other Journals & Devotionals by this author:

The Cool of the Day – Journal for times spent with God

got HEALING? Verses for Life

got HOPE? Verses for Life

got WISDOM? Verses for Life

got GRACE? Verses for Life

got JOY? Verses for Life

got PEACE? Verses for Life

got LOVE? Verses for Life

He Hears Us, Prayer Journal *in 4 different colors*

I Have A Star, Dream Journal *in styles for kids, teen, young adult and up.*

I Have A Star, Guided Prayer Journal, *2 styles: Boy or Girl*

J'ai une Etoile, Journal des Reves

Let Her Dream, Dream Journal *in multiple colors*

Men Shall Dream, Dream Journal, *(blue or black)*

My Favorite Prayers (in 4 styles)

My Sowing Journal (in three different colors)

Tengo una Estrella, Diario de Sueños

Wise Counsel Journal

Illustrated children's books by this author:

Big Dog (8-book series)
Do Not Say That to Me
Every Apple
Fluff the Clouds
I Love You All Over the World
Imma Dance
The Jump Rope
Kiss the Sun
The Masked Man
Not During a Pandemic
Push the Wind
Tangled Taffy
What If?
Wiggle, Wiggle; Giggle, Giggle
Worry About Yourself
You Did Not Say Goodbye to Me

www.ingramcontent.com/pod-product-compliance
Lightning Source LLC
Chambersburg PA
CBHW071925020426
42331CB00010B/2722